Grammar for Literacy

Year 3

David Orme

Introduction

The photocopiable pages in this book, and the accompanying teachers' notes, provide support and source material for the DfEE document *Grammar for Writing*. They can also be used independently as a complete course in the essentials of grammar in the context of writing for years 3 to 6.

Principles

Traditionally, grammar has been taught through exercises, usually single sentences illustrating the particular grammatical point. Teachers have found that teaching grammar in this way, without a meaningful context, is unlikely to be as successful as teaching grammar within the context of the children's own reading and writing. However, that approach too has its own problems – waiting for a grammatical point to arise from work in progress makes any systematic teaching of the subject difficult.

   This series attempts to provide the context for looking at grammar by providing a lively selection of short but complete texts – fiction, non-fiction and poetry – which have been specially written to illustrate the key points. The notes provide suggestions for teaching strategies, and a range of writing tasks to reinforce children's understanding. The focus of the activities is entirely on writing; other reinforcement activities, and background for teachers on the grammatical issues, are covered very thoroughly in the *Grammar for Writing* document.

Using the materials

The materials are designed both for whole-class presentation and for group and individual work. The writing activities can be used flexibly – the guided writing should involve a teacher or other adult, and can be done with the whole class or in a group. The independent writing activities are suitable for small groups, children working in pairs, or individuals.

   In some cases additional texts are provided in the teachers' notes, and preparation may be needed before the session starts.

Contents

	Notes for Teachers pages	Photocopiable page
Topic 1: Past and Present Tense Understanding the function of verbs Thinking about verb choice for meaning and impact Understanding the concepts of past and present tense	2-3	32
Topic 2: Question Marks and Exclamation Marks The function and grammar of questions The purposes of exclamation marks	4-5	33
Topic 3: Setting out Speech The conventions of speech punctuation Making dialogue writing more interesting	6-7	34
Topic 4: Using Textual Devices Using headings, symbols and typographical devices	8-9	35
Topic 5: Sentence Structure and Punctuation Understanding what a sentence is Identifying boundaries between separate sentences Writing in complete sentences	10-11	36
Topic 6: Using Paragraphs Organising stories into paragraphs Understanding paragraphing conventions for dialogue	12-13	37
Topic 7: Non-chronological Reports Using commas in lists Writing simple non-chronological reports Making notes to organise and present ideas	14-15	38
Topic 8: Adjectives Identifying adjectives and exploring their function	16-17	39
Topic 9: Singulars and Plurals Extending knowledge of pluralisation Understanding what is meant by a collective noun Identifying nouns that cannot be pluralised	18-19	40
Topic 10: Redundancy Essential and non-essential words Picking out key points Note making	20-21	41
Topic 11: Person and Agreement Knowledge of the first, second and third person, singular and plural Revision of agreement	22-23	42
Topic 12: Pronouns Understanding the functions of personal and possessive pronouns Pronoun/verb agreement	24-25	43
Topic 13: Conjunctions Using conjunctions to build sentences Using long and short sentences	26-27	44
Topic 14: Time Sequences Understanding time sequences	28-29	45
Topic 15: Using Commas Using commas to separate items in a list Using commas to mark grammatical boundaries in sentences	30-31	46

Topic 1 Past and Present Tense

GfW units covered: 1, 2

Objectives: S3, S4, S5 (Term 1)

Grammar or language topics covered:

- Understanding the function of verbs
- Thinking about verb choice for meaning and impact
- Understanding the concepts of past and present tense

Ideally, each topic should be covered in a separate session.

● ●

Session 1

This session should:

★ introduce the concept of a verb if children are unfamiliar with it;

★ discuss its function;

★ discuss its importance in a sentence;

★ show that more than one word can form a verb chain.

Whole class

Read passage 1 *Shipwreck Shock*, which is in narrative form. Point out some of the simpler verbs, e.g. glided, passed, dodged, saw, reached, hoped. Discuss how they tell the reader what the character was doing.

Now point out verbs that show 'being' rather than doing, e.g. knew, was, had. This is a more difficult idea than 'doing'.

Introduce the word 'verb'. Explain that a verb can be thought of as a 'being' word as well as a 'doing' word.

Read two or three sentences without the verb, e.g. 'Jenny down to the wreck', 'A small shoal of fish by', 'Jenny a heap of rocks'. Discuss why the sentences no longer make sense.

Look at verb chains such as 'was fading', 'would see'. Explain that both words are needed to complete the verb.

Shared writing

The independent writing activity is to continue the story. Work together on three further sentences explaining how Jenny or Ben managed to stop Sarah waving her arms, and avoid the shark attack. Discuss the choice of verbs used. Include 'being' verbs, e.g. 'Ben was very frightened'. Discuss further verbs for the remainder of the story to provide a range of choices that will create tension and excitement.

Independent writing

Continue the story of the exploration of the wreck.

Session 2

This session should cover:

★ interesting/appropriate verb choice.

 Note: a thesaurus would be a useful resource for this activity.

Whole class

Reread passage 1. Decide how many verbs could be substituted by the verb 'to swim', e.g. 'Jenny swam down', 'the shark was swimming slowly towards them'.

Discuss why the author has used a range of words. Are they better choices? Why?

Discuss synonyms for the words 'saw' and 'see', e.g. spotted, noticed, and why these are strong verbs.

Review word choice in the pieces of extended writing from session 1.

Shared writing

Discuss a range of synonyms for a simple action such as 'walked', e.g. strolled, hurried, crept, wandered, marched. Ask a child to 'perform' the described action. Write a sentence for each word, giving it a context.

Work on a 'scaffold' to support the independent writing, e.g. where, why and when it was moving.

Independent writing

Write a short piece of action text describing the movement of an animal or person. Less able children could be provided with a 'prompt list' of verbs.

Session 3

This session should cover:

★ interesting/appropriate verb choice.

Whole class

Read passage 2 *The Great White Shark*, and contrast it with passage 1. Ask children for the differences and similarities, e.g. sharks feature in both but the first tells a story and the second gives information.

Point out and discuss the verbs in the passage, e.g. grows, preys, uses. Contrast with a sentence from passage 1.

Introduce the idea of past and present tense, i.e. one is happening now, the other in the past.

Change a sentence from passage 1 into the present tense, e.g. 'Jenny glides'. What effect does this have? Change a sentence from passage 2 into the past tense, e.g. 'grew to a length'. What effect does this have?

Shared writing.

Write a short piece of informational writing on dinosaurs. Discuss why this should be written in the past tense.

Independent writing

A short piece of informational writing using the present tense about a simple subject, e.g. themselves, a friend, an animal. Less able children would benefit from a writing scaffold, e.g. likes, dislikes, appearance, character.

Topic 2

Question Marks and Exclamation Marks

GfW unit covered: 3

Objective: S6 (Term 1)

Grammar or language topics covered:

- The function and grammar of questions
- The purposes of exclamation marks

The materials should be covered in three sessions.

- -

Session 1

This session should cover:

★ the function of the question mark;

★ how questions can be used.

 Whole class

Read passage 1 *A Fan of Fudge*, and discuss it generally. Who is speaking? Why is it written in this way? (i.e. is it a diary or journal, or is the narrator telling somebody about the experience?) Why is the final sentence surprising and funny?

If children are unfamiliar with the question mark, introduce it now and identify it in the passage. Away from the text, give out a list of questions and statements – two or three of each – without punctuation, and work with the class to identify which are questions. (Note: in speech questions are indicated by emphasis and a rising cadence in the voice – this can be discussed and used to help identify the questions.)

Now look at the questions in the extract. Divide these into questions spoken by the reporter and Billy Rash, and the unanswered questions at the start of the extract.

 Shared writing

Work together on questions that might be in the mind of a pupil starting at a new school, e.g. 'What will the teachers be like?', 'Will I make friends?' and so on. Alternatively, supply a range of answers, e.g. 'The teachers are lovely!' and ask children to identify the questions.

Now work on two or three questions that a teacher might ask a pupil newly arrived in their class.

 Extended writing

Ask children to choose a 'natural' object or idea such as the sun, the wind, a rainbow etc. Ask them to create a list of questions for their chosen object or idea, e.g. 'Why are you so hot?', 'Where do your colours come from?'

This session should cover:

★ the function of the exclamation mark.

Whole class

Identify exclamation marks. Explain that they are used to show exclamations (words that are not part of a sentence such as 'Bother!'), or to emphasise surprising, exciting, frightening or funny things. Read those parts of the passage again that use exclamation marks, showing that the way the words are spoken is the best indicator of the need for an exclamation mark. It is important that children grasp the idea that punctuation is first and foremost a tool to aid reading, in terms of pacing, stress, intonation, and so on.

Shared writing

Work on a short piece of first-person writing about a crisis, e.g. missing the bus, losing some money, an escaped pet.

Independent writing

Either ask children to extend the piece of shared writing, or (a more difficult activity) provide answers for the questions written in session 1, using exclamation marks where appropriate. If this activity is chosen, model it first in shared writing.

Session 3

This session should cover:

★ understanding of question marks and exclamation marks.

Whole class

Ask children to look at passage 2 *Breaking in*, but do not read it aloud at this point. Ask the class to identify any places where a question mark or exclamation mark could be used.

Now read the passage aloud, using appropriate intonation and emphasis. Again, ask children to put their hands up when they think there should be a question mark, and clap when they think there should be an exclamation mark.

Mark the punctuation on a whole-class version of the text. Continue the extract for two more sentences, one ending in a question mark, the other an exclamation mark.

Shared writing

Use the material generated in the first session to begin a piece of writing on the topic 'My first day at school'. The first part should be based on questions, e.g. 'Before I got to school I was worried. Would they like me?' The second section should answer the first: 'It was great! I loved it!' etc.

Independent writing

Ask children to continue with the writing begun in the shared writing session.

Topic

3 Setting out Speech

GfW units covered: 4, 16
Objectives: S7, S8 (Term 1), S4 (Term 3)
Grammar or language topics covered:

- The conventions of speech punctuation
- Making dialogue writing more interesting by finding alternatives to 'said'

Session 1

This session should cover:

★ differentiation between what is spoken and what is not spoken in a passage;

★ speech marks.

Whole class
Read passage 1 *Panic Stations (1)* aloud so that the class can gain the sense of it.

Ask the children to mark up the dialogue in first few lines of the extract, using one colour for Tess and a different colour for Mum.

Ask two children to perform the extract, with the teacher acting as narrator.

Discuss why the words 'said Mum' etc are not highlighted, i.e. they are not spoken.

Point out the speech marks, and discuss their function.

Shared writing
Work on three simple sentences using the 'said' formula.

Independent writing
Ask children to extend the piece of shared writing with three further sentences extending the conversation, perhaps using a thesaurus and preparing with a spelling bank activity.

Session 2

This session should cover:

★ how a new speaker requires a new paragraph;

★ the use of the capital letter to introduce speech;

★ how punctuation marks 'attached' to the words spoken are written inside the

speech marks.

Whole class
Reread passage 1 and introduce these topics. The DfEE's *Grammar for Writing* (*GfW*) highlights the importance of paragraphing to aid intelligibility, and this should be the starting point. Children who find the aspects of punctuation difficult will need additional practice to reinforce their understanding (see Topic 6 page 12).

Shared writing

Use the sentences produced in the shared writing from session 1. Fill out with non-spoken material as in the opening of passage 1 to make an interesting narrative. Keep to the 'said . . .' formula for the time being. Ensure the paragraphing/punctuation rules are applied.

Independent writing

Ask children to carry out the same task with the independent writing produced in session 1.

Session 3

This session should cover how to describe dialogue in more interesting ways by

★ using alternatives to said;

★ using adverbs;

★ rearranging the order of the sentence.

Whole class

Read passage 2 *Panic Stations (2)* and compare it with passage 1. Why is it more interesting?

Find examples of verbs that are alternatives to 'said' e.g. 'wailed'. Look for examples of rearranged sentences and discuss the effect. Find examples of words used to show how the words were spoken, e.g. 'firmly'. Identify places where the 'said' verb has been missed out completely, because the reader already knows who is speaking. With an able group, discuss the ambiguity of 'Mum looked round and pointed' and why the alternative version is better.

Shared writing

Use these ideas to make the pieces of shared writing from sessions 1 and 2 more interesting.

Independent writing.

Ask children to carry out the same task with the independent writing produced in sessions 1 and 2.

Topic 4 Using Textual Devices

GfW unit covered: 5

Objective: S9 (Term 1)

Grammar or language topics covered:

- The use of headings
- Typographical devices
- Underlining and capitalisation
- Symbols

● ●

Session 1

This session should cover:

★ the use of headings and sub-headings in information text

★ ways in which headings can be differentiated from body text.

Whole class

Read passage 1, *Tigers*. Discuss the meaning of the phrase 'information text'. Ask the children to highlight the main heading 'Tigers' in one colour and the sub-headings in another. Discuss their function in introducing the overall topic of the text, and the individual topics of each paragraph.

Discuss the appearance of the headings and sub-headings – bold/enlarged text, italics. Why is it important that they stand out? Why does the main heading need to be different from the paragraph sub-headings? What alternatives could be used, e.g. colour? (You could explain that colour printing is more expensive, where cost is an issue.)

Shared writing

Devise a heading and sub-headings for an article on an individual child, e.g. what he/she looks like, where he/she lives, what he/she likes doing.

Independent writing

Ask children to use the shared writing as a template to write about themselves, using first person/present tense.

Session 2

This session should cover other devices such as

★ bold type

★ italics

★ symbols

★ devices in longhand: underlining, capitals

Whole class

Look again at passage 1. Point out the devices listed above and discuss the ways in which they are used (e.g. bullets highlight a list of items, italics are used for sub-headings and bold type identifies the different groups of tiger). If possible, using a word processing program with the class, find the location of the devices featured in the passage.

Look at further examples of non-fiction text using different typographical conventions. Discuss which of these devices could be used in handwritten work. What could be used instead of bold/italic type? The children might think of using highlighters, different-coloured inks, larger-sized writing, writing in capitals, underlining and so on.

Shared writing

Work together on using some of these ideas to present the first paragraph of passage 1 in long hand.

Independent writing

Ask children to explore ways in which they could make use of some of the devices discussed in their piece of writing about themselves from session 1.

Session 3

This session should cover:

★ how italics are used to indicate stressed words in fiction text;

★ how capital letters can indicate loud voices;

★ the importance of moderation in the use of these devices.

Whole class

Read passage 2 *Wheelie Big Trouble*, taking care to stress italicised words and extra volume for words in capitals.

Discuss how italics are used and the meaning of the word 'stress'. Discuss the italicised words (*by Order*) that perform a different function.

Reread the passage, this time not stressing italicised words, and discuss the difference.

Discuss how the capital letters are used to indicate 'a very loud voice'.

Ask the class why they think the sign is set out in the way it is.

Discuss other words in the passage that could be stressed with italics and the effect that over-using them would have.

Explain to the class that underlining is used in handwritten text as an alternative to italics.

Shared writing

Create two sentences with the class showing two examples of underling to indicate stress, e.g. "I'm absolutely <u>fed up</u>," said Tess. "Billy has got me in trouble <u>again</u>!"

Independent writing

Ask the children to continue with the piece of shared writing, but tell them that they are rationed to just one more use of underlining; they will have to use it carefully!

Sentence Structure and Punctuation

GfW units covered: 6, 12

Objectives: S10, S11, S12 (Term 1); S8 (Term 2)

Grammar or language topics covered:

- Gaining an understanding of what a sentence is
- Identifying boundaries between separate sentences
- Understanding the conventions of capital letters and full stops in sentences
- Identifying other uses for the capital letter
- Writing in complete sentences

Session 1

This session should cover:

★ understanding what a sentence is;

★ understanding that a subject and a verb are essential parts of a sentence;

★ identifying individual sentences within a text.

Whole class

Before showing the passage *London Snow* to the class, explain that you are going to read one paragraph and that the class are going to guess how many sentences there are in it.

Read out paragraph one, giving a clear pause between sentences, then ask the children how many sentences there were, and how they knew. Now show them the passage, and discuss their guesses. This activity should demonstrate that the first way to define a sentence is by listening – it sounds complete.

Now look at the first sentence. Read it out, missing out first the subject – 'opened the door' and then the verb – 'Ravi the door'. Discuss why these do not make sense.

Introduce the idea of a subject – someone or something that does something. (*GfW* proposes the term 'actor' – you could explain that this is the person or thing who performs the action.) Pick out three or four sentences from the passage and identify the subject.

Now introduce the idea of the action – the subject needs to do something! Refer back to the work in Topic 1 on verbs, and identify verbs in selected sentences.

Finally, look at the remainder of the sentence – the ending, which rounds it off – Ravi (subject) opened (verb) the door (ending).

Shared writing

Work with the class to produce three simple sentences showing subject and verb. At least one should be without an object, e.g. 'Ravi woke up'.

Independent writing

Ask children to write three sentences showing a subject and verb. Provide scissors, and ask them to cut up the sentences into subject, verb and ending. In groups, recombine these to make 'silly' sentences, e.g. The snail/ate/the moon. (Alternatively, the sentences could be prepared in advance by the teacher.)

This session should cover:

★ reinforcement of work in session 1 on sentence structure;

★ use of full stop and capital letters to indicate a sentence;

★ extended sentences.

Whole class

Return briefly to passage 1, and highlight capital letters and full stops used to demarcate sentences. Remind the class of this important rule.

Work with the class on some or all of the cloze activity in passage 2. The spaces require a subject, a verb or an ending. Use the first sentence to show that there can be more than one person/thing making up the subject. There is more than one possibility for some spaces, e.g. the street, our street, Nelson Street.

Shared writing

In the independent writing activity, children are to write a short instructional text showing how to make a snowman, using exactly five sentences. Model this activity now, producing a set of notes indicating what is to feature in each sentence.

Independent writing

Ask children to work up the snowman notes into five correctly-written sentences.

Session 3

This session should cover:

★ other uses of the capital letter.

Whole class

Reread passage 1, underlining words other than sentence openers that have capital letters, e.g. Ravi, January, London, Mr Smith.

Introduce the idea of 'naming' or proper nouns for people, places, months and days of the week.

Return to the shared writing produced in session 2. Was this rule followed correctly?

Work together to create a class guide to capital letters, showing when they are used. Include other uses, such as initials, and to show loudness (Topic 4) and as used in headings, signs, notices and so on.

Shared writing

Ask the class to work on a days of the week poem, using a structure such as this:

On Monday I wanted to go to London,
But the train driver was on strike!

On Tuesday I asked for my pocket money,
But Mum just shouted "WHO BROKE THE WINDOW?"

Each day should include one further example of capital letter use.
Produce a class poem based on this structure as a model for the independent writing.

Independent writing

Ask children to write their own poems based on this model. A more ambitious structure would be to use months of the year instead of days of the week.

Topic

6 Using Paragraphs

GfW unit covered: 8
Objective: T16 (Term 1)
Grammar or language topics covered:

- Organisation of stories into paragraphs
- Paragraphing conventions for dialogue

• •

Session 1

This session should cover:

★ the function of paragraphs in a narrative.

Whole class

Read and show passage 1 *The Story of the Escaped Tiger*. Discuss the sections that the narrative naturally falls into, i.e. (1) setting the scene, (2) introducing and describing the characters, (3) the action of the story, (4) the surprising conclusion.

Discuss the decisions the writer made about when to start a new paragraph, e.g. when the subject or time changes, when a new character is introduced or when an action begins. Emphasise that, in a longer story, these parts of the narrative may have more than one paragraph devoted to them, i.e. each character may have a paragraph, or there might be two or more aspects to the scene setting.

Discuss (but not in detail at this stage) how the paragraph structure is disrupted with the introduction of dialogue.

Shared writing

As a class, produce an opening paragraph setting the scene for a story that contrasts with the one in the passage, e.g. a busy street, on the moon, under the sea.

Independent writing

Ask students to write a further paragraph in which they introduce two characters to the story.

Session 2

This session should cover:

★ revision of how to set out dialogue in paragraphs;

★ revision of punctuation.

Whole class

This session should revise work first encountered in Topic 3 on setting out dialogue. It was suggested there that, if children found it difficult to grasp all the aspects of the topic, learning to give a new speaker a new paragraph would be a good start.

Look again at passage 1, from the moment the little girl appears. Discuss the new speaker/new line rule and look at the way in which the direct speech is punctuated, including revision of question marks and capital letters.

It is not made explicit who speaks the last piece of dialogue. Who says this? How does the reader know? Why did the author leave out the name? (Missing out the name speeds up the action at a 'fast' point in the narrative.)

Shared writing

Select two characters from the independent writing produced in session 1 and produce a short, correctly set out piece of dialogue.

Independent writing

Ask children to carry out the same task with the characters they created in session 1.

Session 3

This session should cover:

★ developing paragraphs for stories.

Whole class

Discuss the narrative events in the picture story sequence. Compare with the story structure in passage 1.

Discuss how significant events – e.g. the castaway sees the boat – can be placed at the end of a paragraph to give a cliffhanger effect, e.g. 'Despairingly, Bill looked out to sea one last time. He stared in astonishment. A sail!'

Identify which sections of the story would contain dialogue. What might the characters be saying to each other? Establish the names of the two characters.

Shared writing

Work together to produce the next paragraph of the story.

Independent writing

Ask children to produce the remaining paragraphs. This task could involve groups, pairs or individuals tackling just one paragraph to create composite stories. This activity may need to spread into an extended writing session.

Topic

7 Non-chronological Reports

GfW units covered: 7, 9
Objectives: S13, T23 (Term 1)
Grammar or language topics covered:

- Use of commas in lists
- Writing simple non-chronological reports
- Making notes to organise and present ideas

●●

Session 1

This session should cover:

★ the main features of non-chronological reports.

Whole class

Discuss with the class why some non-fiction needs to be written in chronological order, e.g. instructions, and why. (Refer back to the work done on snowmen in Topic 5.) Now talk about non-fiction where this does not matter, and why. (Refer back to the extract on tigers in Topic 4.)

Read passage 1 *All about Kites* and ask children which of these two types it is. What type of text is the final paragraph? How does it change at this point?

Discuss the content and purpose of each of the four paragraphs in the extract, and provide a heading for each. Talk about the importance of the first 'overview' paragraph.

Shared writing

Discuss and produce paragraph headings and the overview paragraph for a familiar topic, e.g. our school, looking after a pet, where we live.

Independent writing

Ask children to complete the piece of shared writing. Able pupils may prefer to tackle a topic of their own choosing.

Session 2

This session should cover:

★ note making.

Whole class

Compare passage 1 with the same information in note form in passage 2. Discuss the key similarities and differences. Is any information missed out? Which passage is most helpful, and why? How could the notes be used?

Explain that notes can made from an extended text, as in passage 2, or the reverse can apply – a passage can be written from the notes, which may have come from a non-text source, e.g. a television programme.

Shared writing

Create a set of notes from the text produced in session 1.

Independent writing

Ask children to use the set of notes on windsurfing (passage 3) to create a non-chronological report, working out appropriate paragraph headings. This could be done as a group activity. Before they begin, explain the meaning of keel (a flat piece of the board that sticks into the water to stop the board drifting sideways) and boom (a pole fixed to the bottom of a sail to keep it stretched).

Session 3

This session should cover:

★ the use of commas in lists.

Whole class

Read again the second paragraph of passage 1. Point out that the items in the list of kite shapes are separated by commas but that the last item of the list, introduced by the words 'or even', does not have a comma before it. Read the sentence aloud and ask children why they think this is so. Discuss why the writer has used the phrase 'or even' rather than a simple 'and'.

Shared writing

Create list sentences along the lines of the one in the passage, e.g. 'the road was busy with buses, cars, motor-bikes, vans and lorries.'

Independent writing

Children should use one of the list sentences in a short non-chronological report, using the various features of these reports that have been discussed.

15

Topic

8 Adjectives

GfW unit covered: 10
Objectives: S2, S3 (Term 2)
Grammar or language topics covered:

- Identifying adjectives
- Exploring their function
- Experimenting with a range of adjectives

• •

Session 1

This session should cover:

★ identifying adjectives;

★ understanding their function.

Whole class
Read the poem *December*. Point out the adjectives busy, crowded, tired, brightly-coloured and weary from the first stanza.

Discuss the function of these words (to describe) and identify the nouns they qualify. Explain that these words are called adjectives and that they describe nouns. Play the adjective game by showing a familiar classroom object and asking for ten adjectives to describe it – silly ones not excluded!

Identify adjectives that come before a noun (weary) or after a verb (crowded).

Now read the whole poem. Discuss how the poet has used the same adjectives to describe different things. Would it have been better to think of new adjectives? Why not?

Shared writing
Write the first two sentences of a prose description of a crowded city scene, using a range of interesting adjectives.

Independent writing
Ask children to continue the descriptive writing, underlining the adjectives once the writing is completed.

Session 2

This session should cover:

★ experimenting with a range of adjectives.

Whole class
Read passage 2 *Hot Stuff*, and ask the children what they think of it. The class should find that the repetition of the word 'hot' makes for dull reading.

Now compare this with passage 3 *In the Heat*. Highlight the adjectives that replace 'hot' in one colour and any other replaced adjectives in another colour.

Shared writing

Ask children to imagine the weather in the town has changed and start work on a new passage, e.g. 'The day was wet. In the damp city, people looked at their dripping gardens and hoped for sunshine.'

Independent writing

Ask children to complete and extend the passage under the new weather conditions. Able pupils could start with a weather type of their own choosing.

Session 3

This session should cover:

★ further work on finding more interesting adjectives;

★ finding alternatives to adjectives such as stronger nouns or descriptive comparisons.

Whole class

Return to passage 2. Find an example where an adjective ('hotter') is replaced in passage 3 by a descriptive phrase ('as if they were in an oven').

Find a 'hot' that has not been replaced (hot dog) and ask why this has not been changed – it is part of a noun in this case.

Find replacements that are not synonyms for hot – e.g. 'tanned' and discuss why this change was made, i.e. readers did not need to be told that the people were hot.

Discuss stronger nouns that could be used in the place of some adjectives, i.e. sunbathers instead of tanned people, scorcher instead of sunny day.

Shared writing

Develop further sentences for the passage 3, employing strong nouns and interesting comparisons rather than further adjectives.

Independent writing

Children should work on passage 4 *The Big Chill*, finding new adjectives for those underlined and interesting words for the gaps. Able children might find stronger nouns or comparisons to use instead.

Topic 9

Singulars and Plurals

GfW unit covered: 11
Objectives: S4, S5 (Term 2)
Grammar or language topics covered:

- Extend knowledge of pluralisation
- Identify which words change and which do not when changing from singular to plural
- Understand what is meant by a collective noun
- Identify nouns that cannot be pluralised

Session 1

This session should cover:

★ pluralisation of nouns by adding 's';

★ irregular plurals.

Whole class
Read the two passages The Frog's Adventure and The Frogs' Adventure and ask the children to identify the key difference between them. They will see that there is one of each animal in the first passage, two of each in the second.

Point out examples of plurals formed by adding 's' (frog, sparrow, garden).Introduce the terms 'singular' and 'plural' and define with examples of objects in the classroom.

Now identify irregular plurals from the extract – sheep, calves, factories, mice, children. Include 'leaves' and identify its singular form.

Discuss categories of plurals, including examples not in the passage:
Words ending in 's'.
Words that don't change at all (sheep, deer, fish)
Words ending in 'f' or 'fe' (calf, leave, loaf, thief, wolf, half, knife)
Words ending in 'y' (factory, lady, army, fly)
Words that change several of their letters (mouse, foot)
(Note: other irregulars, such as 'o' 'x' or 's' endings are probably best left for another time.)

Shared writing
Introduce the first few lines of a nonsense poem based on plurals:

1 thief stole a loaf
2 thieves stole two loaves
1 mouse hid in a factory,
2 mice . . .   and so on.

Independent writing
Children should continue the poem using plural combinations of their own.

This session should cover:

★ agreement.

Whole class

Return to the passages. This time, point out verbs and pronouns that change: was/were, he/they, its/their, him/them and so on.

First run through the pronouns, making a simple table:

Just one	More than one
I	we
he, she	they

Work on creating simple sentences showing these words in context, then focus on constructions including the verb to be: I was running/ you were running/ they were running.

The most important skill children can develop is to know when the agreement sounds wrong, and plenty of oral work will help.

Shared writing

Introduce the idea of a 'but' poem, e.g.

I was right but you were wrong!
I was winning but you were losing!

Independent writing

Ask children to extend the poems individually, making their poems as funny as possible.

This session should cover:

★ collective nouns;

★ words that don't pluralise.

Whole class

Highlight the word 'flock' from the passage, and discuss its meaning. Discuss what is meant by collective nouns and ask children to provide the appropriate collective noun for a range of creatures, e.g. a swarm of bees, a herd of cows, a class of children, a fleet of ships.

Now introduce the idea of nouns with no singular, e.g. pliers, spectacles, thanks, trousers, shorts, underpants, tights, tongs, mumps. Discuss why these do not have plurals, i.e. they are, in one sense or another, plural anyway.

Shared writing

Discuss and invent humorous collective nouns for a range of creatures, e.g. a hop of frogs.

Independent writing

Use the idea of humorous collective nouns for a simple poem about an animal parade, e.g.

A chatter of monkeys swung from the trees,
A buzz of wasps looked for someone to sting. . .

Or, ask children to write a humorous poem on singular objects that have no singular, e.g.

What's a measle?
A measle is what you find
On someone who's barely ill. . .

Topic

10 Redundancy

GfW unit covered: 13
Objective: S9 (Term 2)
Grammar or language topics covered:

- Essential and non-essential words
- Picking out key points
- Note making

- -

Session 1

This session should cover:

★ words we can do without.

Whole class
Write up the first sentence of passage 1 *Too Many Words*!, and read it out. Cover each word in turn and see if the sentence makes sense without it.

Look for examples of groups of words that could be cut (e.g. 'is a word that', 'whether they are') while single words in the group could not.

Discuss why the various words and expressions are redundant, e.g. the reader knows that 'amphibian' is a word.

Discuss why using unnecessary words makes writing more difficult to read and understand.

Shared writing
Work together on an 'ideal' version of the first sentence.

Independent writing
Without giving children access to the second passage, ask them to discuss in groups the next two sentences and produce shortened versions.

Session 2

This session should cover:

★ tautology.

Whole class
Read through passage 1 once more. Highlight two or three examples of words that simply repeat the meaning of other words, e.g. 'In the early stages' – 'at the beginning of their lives', 'slowly' – 'gradually', 'full-grown' – 'adult', 'tiny' – 'small'.

Read the passage again and ask children to identify any further examples.

Discuss any further examples of unnecessary words that 'state the obvious', e.g. 'the water they came from'. Now read through passage 2 *Frogs (1)*. Discuss the changes that have been made, and why. Is this passage easier to read and understand?

Shared writing

Work on the last paragraph of passage 2. Is it still too long? Could it be made even shorter? Work together on a shorter version, then compare it with the final paragraph of passage 3 *Frogs (2)*. Has anything important been missed out? Has the writer used one word (e.g. spring) where more than one has been used in passage 2?

Independent writing

Use the information in the final paragraph of passage 2 as the basis for an extended piece of fictional writing, perhaps based on the character(s) met in Topic 9. Before the children begin, explain to them that extended descriptions in fiction can make writing more interesting, though they should still try to avoid telling people what they already know or using two or more words with the same meaning.

Session 3

This session should cover:

★ picking out key points.

Whole class

Return to passage 1. Ask the class to identify key facts about frogs, i.e. they live in water and on land, their bodies change, they eat small creatures, they hibernate. Write these out as a bulleted list.

Turn to passage 3. Compare this with the bulleted list – has anything important been missed out of either text?

Shared writing

Rewrite passage 3 as a set of notes. For each paragraph produce a heading (e.g. life cycle, feeding, hibernation). Then bullet the individual facts under each heading. Compare with the original bulleted list. How has it been improved?

Independent writing

Ask children to produce a similar set of notes on another animal they are familiar with, e.g. a migrating bird.

Topic

11 Person and Agreement

GfW unit covered: 14

Objectives: S10, S11 (Term 2)

Grammar or language topics covered:

- Knowledge of the first, second and third person, singular and plural
- How the first, second and third person are used in writing
- Revision of agreement

● ●

Session 1

This session should cover:

★ first and third person.

Whole class

Read passages 1 and 2 *Following Behind (1)* and *(2)* and discuss the main differences. Explain that passage 1 is written in the first person, using 'I'. 'I' can be used for autobiographical writing, or for writing where the author 'pretends' to be someone. The story is written from their point of view.

Third-person writing is written about a character, such as Susan in passage 2. Highlight the words that have been changed in the two passages and remind children that words change to match the subject of the sentence. How would it change if the subject were a boy rather than Susan?

Shared writing

Complete passage 2 based on the events of passage 1.

Independent writing

Passage 4 *Being Followed* is written in the first person from the point of view of the person being pursued. Ask children to complete this, based on the information in passage 1.

Session 2

This session should cover:

★ writing in the third person plural;

★ writing in the first person plural.

Whole class

Read passage 3, identifying that there are now two characters involved. Discuss the differences between passages 2 and 3.

Discuss the further option of first person plural, using 'we'. Discuss when this might be used in writing, e.g. a description of a class outing.

Shared writing

Complete passage 3 using the first person plural, based on the information in passage 1.

Independent writing

Ask the children to work on a short recount written in the first person plural, e.g. a group outing, an account of a football team.

Session 3

This session should cover:

★ writing in the second person.

Whole class

Read the part of a sentence that makes up passage 5 *How to Follow Someone*. Explain that the word 'you' is used when you are speaking directly to someone, either to give instructions, ask questions, give opinions about them ('you are crazy!') or tell them what they are doing/or did ('you were hiding in that doorway').

Look at the work done on passage 4 (session 1) and see if the second person has been used – remember that the word 'you' needs to be the subject of the sentence. Explain that the second person is mostly used for asking questions and giving instructions.

Shared writing

Work together on a new extension of passage 4. This time the person followed asks a series of questions about why he is being followed.

Independent writing

Continue passage 5. Children should use ideas of their own as well as ideas from passage 1.

Topic

12 Pronouns

GfW unit covered: 15
Objectives: S2, S3 (Term 3)
Grammar or language topics covered:

- Identify and understand the functions of pronouns
- Personal pronouns and possessive pronouns
- Pronoun/verb agreement

• •

Session 1

This session should cover:

★ identifying pronouns;

★ understanding their function.

Whole class
This session is based on the passages previously encountered in Topic 11.

Reread passage 2, pointing out the pronouns he, she, it and passage 3, pointing out they he, it. Ask the children which person or people they stand for, and write a table:

she = Susan   they = Susan and Mike   he = the person they are following   it = the stone

Introduce the word 'pronoun' and explain its function, i.e. it takes the place of a noun and means that you don't need to repeat the noun itself.

Reread passage 1. 'I' is a pronoun – do we know who 'I' stands for? Explain that here it stands for the writer of the passage.

Shared writing
Begin a short narrative involving two people – make and female – with the class. Ensure that the words he, she and they are included. Discuss what will happen next.

Independent writing
Ask children to continue the writing begun in the shared writing session.

This session should cover:

★ possessive pronouns;

★ agreement.

Whole class

Return briefly to passage 2 of Topic 11. Point out the appearances of the word 'her'. Explain that 'her' is used (1) as the object of the sentence, i.e. when something is being done to her. He saw *she* is wrong; (2) To show that something belongs to her - her foot.

Work together to find matching words for he (his), I (me, my), they (their, them), you (your).

Shared writing

Begin a piece of dialogue in which a group of children have an argument. Use pronouns from the list.

Independent writing

Ask children to extend the writing. Explain that they will score a point every time they use a word from the pronoun list.

This session should cover:

★ agreement;

★ revision of pronouns.

Whole class

Read together passage 1 of Topic 12 – *The Fish Family (1)*. Discuss why the passage sounds awkward. The class should be able to tell you it is because no pronouns have been used.

Discuss appropriate pronouns for the first paragraph.

Shared writing

As a class, rewrite passage 2, filling in the gaps.

Independent writing

Ask the children work on passage 3 *Charlie's Gang*, finding an appropriate pronoun for each space.

Topic 13 Conjunctions

GfW unit covered: 17
Objective: S5 (Term 3)
Grammar or language topics covered:

- Use of conjunctions to build sentences
- Use of long and short sentences

• •

Session 1

This session should cover:

★ identifying simple conjunctions;

★ joining two sentences.

Whole class
This session focuses on using simple conjunctions such as 'and', 'but', and 'so' to join sentences.

Read through passage 1 *Behind You!*, ensuring that children grasp the gist of the story.

Point out the words 'but', (sentence 1), 'and' (sentence 3), 'so' (twice in paragraph 3), 'and' (paragraph 4), 'so' (final sentence).

Explain that these words link shorter sentences, and break down the relevant sentences to illustrate this, e.g. 'At last she agreed that they could open the airlock', 'The crew rushed out'.

Shared writing
Work through passage 2 *Making Friends*, linking the sentences in pairs using 'and', 'but' and 'so', e.g. 'Professor Ming was rather frightened but the alien turned out to be friendly.'

Independent writing
Ask children to continue passage 1, this time with unfriendly aliens. Explain that they should use 'and', 'but' and 'so' at least once each to link the sentences.

Session 2

This session should cover:

★ using conjunctions to create more complex sentences.

Whole class
Read passage 1 again. This time the focus is on joining clauses with a conjunction at the beginning.

Break down some of the complex sentences into simple sentences, e.g. 'They waited. Tim took photographs out of the window' , 'It looked quiet outside. The professor had warned them...'

Now discuss how these sentences are joined, identifying conjunctions such as because, if, although.

Shared writing

Turning to passage 2, this time build complex sentences starting with a conjunction. The children will have to identify other possible conjunctions, e.g. 'When the crew came back, they found. . .'. Try combining different pairs of sentences, too, e.g. 'because it wasn't working, the alien gave up'.

Independent writing

Ask children to redraft their independent writing from session 1, this time beginning the sentences with an appropriate conjunction.

Session 3

This session should cover:

★ long and short sentences.

 Whole class

The danger of focusing on conjunctions is that children assume that longer sentences are in some way 'better' than shorter ones, which is not necessarily the case.

Reread passage 1 from Topic 1, which illustrates long and short sentences. Point out the simple sentences and complex sentences. Talk about how writers mix long and short sentences, to give variety in their writing.

Discuss how, as the story becomes more action-packed (when the shark appears), the sentences tend to become shorter – short sentences can be used to build tension in a narrative.

 Shared writing

Work on a second redraft of one of the pieces of independent writing produced in previous sessions. This time, work on breaking up the complex sentences to create a more exciting read. Conclude with an exciting reading of the passage so that the children can hear the effect of long and short sentences for themselves.

 Independent writing

Ask children to produce a more extended narrative, using a range of short and long sentences.

Topic 14 — Time Sequences

GfW unit covered: 18
Objective: S6 (Term 3)
Grammar or language topics covered:

• Understanding of time sequences

• •

Session 1

This session should cover time sequences:

★ used in narrative;

★ used in recount.

 Whole class

Read through passage 1 *A Walk in the Dark*. Identify the first thing that happened ('the cat pushed through the cat flap') and the last ('the disappointed cat turned for home').

Read out an alternative version using 'then' as much as possible, e.g. 'the cat pushed through the cat flap then he stood still for a moment then he sniffed the air . .' Discuss why this version isn't very satisfactory.

Highlight words and phrases that tell the reader when the events happened, e.g. as soon as, when, first, next, after that, just then, immediately, etc.

 Shared writing

Begin a short piece of writing involving a different animal, e.g. the story of a potential prey rather than a predator. Use some of the words and phrases highlighted.

 Independent writing

Ask children to complete the narrative using more of the highlighted words and phrases.

Session 2

This session should cover:

★ consolidation of the work on time sequences;

★ introducing further words and phrases showing a time sequence.

 Whole class

Read passage 2 *Henry's Walk Home*. Contrast this with passage 1 and discuss why it isn't so effective. Discuss ways in which passage 2 could be improved.

 Shared writing

Work on an improved version of passage 2, introducing new words and phrases where appropriate, e.g. 'After he had crossed the road . . .', 'Once he had . . .'

Independent writing

Children could continue and complete the shared writing activity. Alternatively, they could write an account of their own involving a sequence of events, perhaps based on a real experience.

Session 3

This session should cover:

★ using time sequences in non-fiction writing.

Whole class

Read together passage 1 from Topic 15 (*The Very Special Pudding*), beginning at 'After tea'.

Identify the words and phrases that show a time sequence.

Discuss activities that need to be done in a particular order (e.g. when making a cake) and those where the order is less critical, (e.g. tidying a bedroom, although children might point out that a floor cannot be vacuum cleaned until everything has been picked up!).

Shared writing

Produce a flow diagram of a sequential task, e.g. following a recipe, building a model, operating a piece of electronic equipment, etc. If possible, build in an 'if . . . then...' construction, with a repeating loop, e.g. 'if the mixture is too wet, then you will need to add more flour'.

Independent writing

Ask children to write out the events of the flow diagram as continuous prose using the words and phrases already encountered.

Topic 15 — Using Commas

GfW units covered: 7, 19
Objectives: S13 (Term 1), S7 (Term 3)
Grammar or language topics covered:

- Using commas to separate items in a list
- Use commas to mark grammatical boundaries in sentences

• •

Session 1

This session should cover:

★ using commas to separate items in a list.

Whole class
Read the first two paragraphs of passage 1 *The Very Special Pudding*. Identify the three lists, i.e. the ingredients, the equipment, the repeated list of ingredients.

Rewrite the list of ingredients without the commas. Discuss how the commas help the reader. Point out that the word 'and' is used before the last item in a list.

Shared writing
Work with the class on sentences involving lists, e.g. 'at school today we did maths,. . .'

Independent writing
Ask children, perhaps working in groups, to write the beginning of a story in which two or three people prepare for an expedition. The writing should list what each person has brought with them. Encourage comic possibilities – one person has brought entirely inappropriate things, or the expedition itself is an unlikely one, e.g. a search for dragons.

Session 2

This session should cover:

★ commas as grammatical boundaries.

Whole class
Return to passage 1. Point out all commas apart from those used in the list. Show how commas can be used to:
- mark off separate information in a sentence, e.g. in sentences 1 and 2.
- mark a dividing point in a sentence, e.g. sentence 1, paragraph 2 'Although she didn't . .'
- separate a clause (part of a sentence which could be a sentence by itself), e.g. 'A tin of nutmeg, which she had got out earlier, was on the table.'

Shared writing
Use ideas from the passage to build new sentences using commas, e.g. 'The guests ate the pudding. They had no idea there was curry powder in it. They enjoyed it very much' could be changed to: 'The guests, who had no idea there was curry powder in the pudding, enjoyed it very much.'

Independent writing

Ask children to work in groups on writing of their own using commas in these ways. (Note: this is a challenging task. A follow-up session in which the work produced is assessed and redrafted would be valuable.)

Session 3

This session should cover:

★ revision of commas in lists using a different format.

Whole class

Perform the poem *What's in the Pud?* with the class.

Discuss the ways the commas are used in the poem to:

• separate items in a list;

• show the reader how to perform the poem.

Discuss the use of brackets around 'please don't sneeze'. Why did the writer need something 'stronger' in addition to the commas?

Why didn't the poet use 'and' before the last item (the dynamite)?

Are the final two lines the same list or a new one? (Point out that commas can be used for lists of actions as well as things.)

Shared writing

Write a recipe book entry for 'exploding pudding'. How will the commas be used?

Independent writing

Create a poem with a list of interesting or comic items, e.g. a magic potion, 'what's in the teacher's secret drawer' or a list of actions, e.g. 'how to catch a dragon', 'how to annoy a teacher'.

Past and Present Tense

Shipwreck Shock

Jenny glided down to the wreck. The light was fading away now, and everything looked grey. A small shoal of fish passed by. She tried to touch them, but they dodged out of the way.

She saw that Ben and Sarah were swimming nearby and she signalled 'I'm OK' to them.

Soon they reached the bed of the sea. Jenny saw a heap of rocks. She remembered them. This was the right way!

At last they reached the wreck. They could see the shape of the old wooden ship clearly, even though seaweed covered it from end to end. The side had a big hole in it. They hoped they might find something exciting inside, maybe even treasure!

Just then Sarah started to wave her arms and point. Jenny looked upwards. Her heart seemed to miss a beat. She saw a huge, dark shape. It was moving slowly towards them.

Only one creature had that outline. There was no doubt about it. It was a great white shark, the deadliest creature in the seas.

Jenny knew that Sarah was doing just the wrong thing. The shark would see her waving arms! They had to stay completely still. If they did, the shark might swim away.

The Great White Shark

The great white shark, sometimes called the man-eating shark, grows to a length of six metres. This creature preys on seals, sea turtles, large fish, and sometimes, people.

The shark uses its sense of smell to find its prey. Its eyes see movement rather than shape and colour. When it finds its prey it circles round it. It often attacks from below, twisting its body round to tear off chunks of flesh.

Great white sharks are a special problem for people in Australia, New Zealand, South Africa and some parts of America. Beaches have lookout towers fitted with special sirens to warn people of shark attacks. Some Australian beaches have nets fixed under the water. These work well in keeping sharks away.

Sharks will attack humans when they are hungry, or annoyed, or when they are defending territory. To a shark the kicking and splashing of legs in the water is like the movement of a wounded fish.

Many people fear sharks, but attacks on humans are rare. Around a hundred people are victims of a shark attack every year. About a quarter of these attacks are fatal.

Remember:

- Stories are usually written in the past tense (e.g. 'Jenny **saw** a heap of rocks').
- Information reports are usually written in the present tense (e.g. 'Many people **fear** sharks').
- Try to choose interesting verbs in your writing.

A Fan of *Fudge*

It was the most exciting day of my life! I had won a competition to meet my favourite group, *Fudge*. I was really nervous. Would I like them when I met them? Would they like me? Would they give me their autographs?

At last the day came. A special car came to pick me up. It was a stretch limo! We got to their hotel and there was a photographer and a reporter waiting for me. The reporter asked me lots of silly questions like "How long had I been a Fudge fan?" and "Why were they my favourite group?"

Then the group came in. We all had our photographs taken. It was brilliant! They were really great. We had a good chat. Suddenly I remembered something. Bother! I'd left my autograph book at home!

It didn't matter though. The group gave me a big poster for my bedroom wall and they all signed it!

"Would you like to have something to eat now?" Billy Rash asked me. I nearly died! Billy is my all-time favourite! So we went off and had burger and fries.

I told them I had really enjoyed the day.

"It was great to meet you," said Billy. "We don't get that many 80-year-old great-grannies coming to see us!"

Breaking in

The man in dark clothes nervously pushed up the window. Would the window be squeaky. Would the alarm go off.

Great. He was inside. He pulled his bag inside the room and flashed on his torch. Had he got the right house. He hoped so.

He looked round the room by the light of the torch. Pictures. Silver ornaments. A big gold clock. Yes. He was in the right place.

Suddenly, he heard a snarl in the darkness. Oh no. Could this mean trouble.

The dog was only small, but she made a lot of noise. She grabbed hold of the man's trousers in her jaws. The man shook his leg, and whispered "Let go" as loud as he dared. But the dog wouldn't.

Just then he heard more noises. Were people waking up. Yes. A light went on in the hall. The door opened. There was a click of a light switch.

"So" boomed a big voice. "Have you lost your key *again*."

"Sorry Dad" he replied.

Remember:

- A question mark should be used at the end of every question.

- An exclamation mark shows something is surprising, sudden, loud or funny.

- It can also be used for a word or phrase that stands by itself and shows your feelings, such as "Bother!", "Brilliant!", "Help!", "Go away!"

Setting out Speech

Panic Stations (1)

It was nearly time to leave for school.

"I can't find my reading book. I've looked everywhere," said Tess.

Mum came into her bedroom. Tess had pulled open her drawers and there were things all over the floor.

"Look at the mess you've made," she said.

"I must take it. Mr Carter gets really cross when we leave them at home," said Tess.

"It's time to go. You must tidy up this mess as soon as you get back," said Mum.

"I promise I will. I'm going to be in big trouble though. Are you sure you haven't seen it?"

Mum looked round and pointed.

"What's that sticking out of your school bag?" said Mum.

"My reading book! I must have packed it yesterday and forgotten!" said Tess.

At last Tess was ready to go to school. When they got to the school car park Tess saw her friend Rachel. She called out to her.

"Hi Rachel," said Tess.

"Hello, Tess, did you have a good weekend?" said Rachel.

They started chatting. Tess's mum waved goodbye and drove off. She didn't notice that the school bag was still on the back seat of the car!

Panic Stations (2)

It was nearly time to leave for school.

"I can't find my reading book," wailed Tess. "I've looked everywhere!"

Mum came into her bedroom. Tess had pulled open her drawers and there were things all over the floor.

Mum looked cross. "Look at the mess you've made," she grumbled.

"I must take it," said Tess. "Mr Carter gets really cross when we leave them at home!"

"It's time to go," said Mum firmly. "You must tidy up this mess as soon as you get back."

"I promise I will," said Tess. "I'm going to be in big trouble though. Are you sure you haven't seen it?"

"What's that sticking out of your school bag?" asked Mum, looking round and pointing.

"My reading book! I must have packed it yesterday and forgotten!" Tess shouted joyfully.

At last Tess was ready to go to school. When they got to the school car park Tess saw her friend Rachel. She called out to her.

"Hi Rachel!"

"Hello, Tess, did you have a good weekend?"

They started chatting. Tess's mum waved goodbye and drove off. She didn't notice that the school bag was still on the back seat of the car!

Remember:

- Put what people actually say inside speech marks (e.g. "Hello!").
- A new speaker needs a new line.
- Don't just use 'said' - there are many other interesting words.

Using Textual Devices

Tigers

Where are they found?

Tigers are found only in Asia, but they cover a wide area from the snows of Siberia to the jungles of India. There are now four groups of tigers:

- **Indian** tiger
- **Chinese** tiger
- **Siberian** tiger
- **Sumatran** tiger.

Balinese, Javanese and **Caspian** tigers are probably now extinct.

What do they look like?

Tigers are the biggest species of cat. They have coloured stripes, which helps to camouflage them. Tigers from India are more brightly coloured than animals from snowy Siberia.

Tigers can grow to reach up to 2.2m long excluding their tail.

Wheelie Big Trouble

Billy and Tess were rowing again.

"I *hate* you!" Billy yelled. "You're always bossing me about, telling me what to do!"

"But why do you have to be so *stupid*?" replied Tess. "You can read, can't you?"

The children were in the park. They were looking at a big sign.

| **No Cycling** |
| *by Order* |

Billy wanted to ride his bike!

"All right, do what you like!" shouted Tess. "Get into trouble if you like! I just don't *care* anymore!"

Billy jumped on his bike and started to do wheelies along the path. Stupid old notice! Who would find out anyway?

Just then they heard a very loud voice.

"CAN'T YOU KIDS READ?"

The park keeper had appeared. Billy jumped off his bike straight away.

The park keeper advanced on them. He glared at Tess.

"I blame you! You are the oldest. You should be more responsible!"

"But I *am* responsible!" Tess started to say. But it was a waste of time. Billy had landed her in trouble again.

Remember:

- Bullet points (•) can be used for lists.
- **Bold type** is useful for headings or picking out important words.
- *Italic* type is used to stress words, for quoting titles of books, and sometimes for headings and sub-headings instead of bold type.
- Capital letters can be used to show SHOUTED words.

Sentence Structure and Punctuation

London Snow

Ravi opened the door. He couldn't believe how much the world had changed. Six centimetres of snow had fallen in the night. The dirty January streets of London were suddenly white. Snow smoothed out the pattern of the tiles on the rooftops and made long cushions along the sills of the windows.

Only the milkman's float had been along the road. Ravi saw the tracks it had made, and the mark of Mr Smith's boots on all the paths. Nearby, he saw the three-toed footprints of a pigeon.

It was Sunday, and Ravi would not be going to school. He went back indoors. In the kitchen, he could hear his parents. They were sharing the job of getting the breakfast ready. Earlier, he had heard them grumbling about the snow.

Ravi decided he would call his best friends, Richard and Rosella. He hoped they would be free to come out into the snow and play.

Summer is good, Ravi thought, but winter can be great too!

"What were you doing out there?" Ravi's mother called. "You'll let all the warm air out of the house!"

The trouble with parents, Ravi thought, is that they don't have any imagination.

Ravi, Richard and _____ decided to build a _____ .

Ravi got a spade out of the shed. They started to _____ .

" _____ going to have the best one in _____ street!" said

_____ .

They set to work. All their parents had been worried that they would _____ ,

but they worked so hard, and got so hot, they thought about taking their coats off!

At last it _____ . They were sure it really was the best _____ in

_____ street. Maybe it was the best in the whole of _____ !

They set off home, planning to come out in the morning before school to _____ .

But the weather was changing. Overnight it started to _____ . By morning all the

snow had been washed away. The _____ had turned into a muddy puddle.

Remember:

- A sentence needs a subject (the person or thing that does something) and a verb (what they do), (e.g. Ravi opened the door).
- A sentence begins with a capital letter and ends in a full stop.
- Proper nouns (names, places, days of the week, months of the year) have capital letters.

The Story of the Escaped Tiger

The old castle frowned down from the jagged mountain top. Hundreds of metres below, a dense green forest seemed to stretch without end. In the air above, golden eagles swooped on the air currents.

Two men were walking across the castle courtyard. One was a young man, perhaps twenty years old. He wore the uniform of a soldier. The other man was older. He had grey hair, a lined face, and walked with a limp. Looking at the two faces, it was easy to guess that they were father and son.

A door opened in the stone wall of the castle. The small figure of a little girl ran out into the sunshine. She wore a red dress and had the same black hair as the young soldier.

"Simon! Father! Come quickly!" shouted the little girl. She looked terrified.

"What is it? What has happened?" asked the older man.

"The tiger has escaped!" wailed the child. "It is eating the servants!"

The two men looked horrified. What a dreadful thing to happen!

"Quick, Simon! There is a dart gun in my study. You can move more quickly than me. Go and fetch it. I'll meet you in the dungeon as soon as I can get there."

The two men rushed off. The little girl laughed to herself. Grown-ups believed everything she told them.

A Story in Four Pictures

Remember:

- Paragraphs are used to make reading easier.
- Each paragraph is about ideas or descriptions that are connected to each other.
- When a new person speaks, a new paragraph is started.

Non-chronological Reports

All about Kites

Kites are made of paper or other material stretched over a frame. They are very popular in Far Eastern countries.

The ninth day of the ninth month is a special kite festival in China called 'Climbing the Heights'. Kites of many kinds are flown, some shaped like birds, butterflies, dragons, fishes or even snakes. Some kites are designed to make musical sounds, to frighten away evil spirits.

Kite flying is also very popular in Japan. Here they are keen on kite fighting. The kites are made with special sharp edges so that they can cut the cords of other kites.

Even flying a simple kite can be very skilful. To fly a kite you should stand with your back to the wind, then, when the kite has been caught by the wind, let out the cord as the kite flies higher. When the kite begins to fall, start pulling the cord in.

Notes on Kites

Very popular in Far Eastern countries, particularly China.
On 9th day of 9th month there is a special kite festival in China.
This is called 'Climbing the Heights'.
Kite shapes include birds, butterflies, dragons, fishes, snakes.
Musical kites are made to frighten evil spirits away.
Kite fighting is popular in Japan.
The kites have sharp edges to cut the cords of the other kites.
Flying a kite is skilful.
Stand with your back to the wind.
Let out cord when the kite pushed up by the wind.
Pull in the cord if the kite starts to sink.

Windsurfing

Windsurfing is a popular water sport invented in the 1960s.
You need:
a **board** with a keel to stop it going sideways
A **rig** - a mast, sail and a boom.
To enjoy windsurfing you first need to know about sailing.
You can windsurf in different directions by moving the position of the sail.
You can tack like a sailing ship. (This means you can windsurf against the direction of the wind by moving in a zigzag.)
Safety is important.
Always wear a lifejacket.
Never windsurf alone.

Remember:

- Start by collecting what you know and what you find out into notes.
- Group the information in your notes into paragraphs.
- Each paragraph covers one part of the subject.
- The first paragraph should explain what the whole topic is about.

Topic 8 Adjectives

December

It's midday, and the busy clock strikes twelve.
The pavements are crowded with tired people
Piled up with brightly-coloured shopping,
Grumbling about the cold,
Stamping their weary feet and breathing out mist,
Wishing their bus would hurry up.

It's midnight, and the weary clock strikes twelve.
The pavements are crowded with snow
Piled up in bright heaps,
Cold and beautiful.
Busy stars twinkle through the mist,
Wishing the moon would come up.

Hot Stuff

The day was hot. In the hot town streets, people watered their dry gardens and hoped for rain. Tools left in the hot sun for too long were too hot to touch. Drivers in their hot cars wound down their windows, but they still got hotter.

On the beaches, hot people licked their cold ice-creams and hoped for another hot day tomorrow. The hot hot-dog man decided to go home. He needed a cold drink!

In the Heat

The day was scorching. In the baking town streets, people watered their thirsty gardens and hoped for rain. Tools left in the burning sun for too long could not be touched. Drivers in their stuffy cars wound down their windows, but they still felt as if they were in an oven.

On the beaches, tanned people licked their refreshing ice-creams and hoped for another sunny day tomorrow. The sweating hot-dog man decided to go home. He needed an iced drink!

The Big Chill

The cold wind blew through the _____ forest, over the cold mountains and down into the cold town. In a small cottage in East Street a small woman sat next to a hot fire. She heard the _____ wind moaning in the chimney, and thought of all the _____ people that were sleeping on the _____ streets that night.

Remember:
- Adjectives are describing words. They come before nouns or after verbs.
- Always choose interesting adjectives, and don't keep repeating the same one.
- Sometimes it's better to choose a more interesting noun (sunbathers) instead of using an adjective (hot people).

Singulars and Plurals

The Frog's Adventure

There was once a frog who was tired of life in the dull pond. He wanted adventure! He asked the animals that came to the pond what the big world was like. But the sheep only knew about its field, the calf only knew about the farmyard, and the mouse was too scared of the bigger animals to say anything at all. The sparrow had travelled the most, and the small brown bird told the frog about the house, the garden and the factory on the other side of the main road.

So one sunny autumn day, just before the leaves on the willow tree near the pond turned yellow, the frog set off on an adventure.

His first problem was crossing the road that ran past the pond. When he reached it he started to hop across, but he didn't know about traffic. Suddenly he heard a squeal, and the world went dark.

Luckily, the wheel had missed him! He heard a door open and saw a child's face looking at him under the car.

"He's all right!" said the child. The frog found himself being picked up and carried back to the pond! The child was pleased to have saved the frog, but the frog was furious!

The Frogs' Adventure

There were once two frogs who were tired of life in the dull pond. They wanted adventure! They asked the animals that came to the pond what the big world was like. But the sheep only knew about their field, the calves only knew about the farmyard, and the mice were too scared of the bigger animals to say anything at all. The flock of sparrows had travelled the most, and the small brown birds told the frog about the houses, the gardens and the factories on the other side of the main road.

So one sunny autumn day, just before the leaves on the willow trees near the pond turned yellow, the frogs set off on an adventure.

Their first problem was crossing the road that ran past the pond. When they reached it they started to hop across, but they didn't know about traffic. Suddenly they heard a squeal, and the world went dark.

Luckily, the wheels had missed them! They heard doors open and saw children's faces looking at them under the car.

"They're all right!" said the children. The frogs found themselves being picked up and carried back to the pond! The children were pleased to have saved the frogs, but the frogs were furious!

Remember:

- Nouns can be singular (one thing) or plural (more than one).
- Most plurals are made by adding an 's' (e.g. frog, frogs).
- Some change in different ways (such as calf, calves).
- If it hisses or buzzes, add es! (e.g. bus, buses)
- Some words don't change at all from singular to plural (e.g. sheep).
- Some nouns are collective nouns and they name a group of things (e.g. flock).

Too Many Words!

Frogs are called amphibians, which is a word that means they are equally at home whether they are on the land or in the water. In the early stages at the beginning of their lives they are called tadpoles, and they spend all of their time in the water of a pond breathing in through gills. Slowly and gradually their bodies change, the gills that they have disappear, and they start to develop lungs. As full-grown adult frogs they spend most of their time out of the water in the open air, but they need to return to the water they came from regularly to stop their bodies drying up.

Frogs feed on tiny, small creatures such as flies, insects, worms and other things like that. They are able to catch insects and flies by flicking out their very sticky tongues very, very fast.

Frogs hibernate right through the cold winter. When the weather becomes cold they bury themselves down in leaves and mud at the bottom of a pond, and wait for the warm weather to come back again.

Frogs (1)

Frogs are amphibians, which means they are equally at home on land or in water. In the early stages of their lives they are called tadpoles, and they live entirely in the water breathing through gills. Slowly their bodies change, the gills disappear, and they develop lungs. As full-grown frogs they spend most of their time out of the water, but they need to return to it regularly to stop their bodies drying up.

Frogs feed on small creatures such as insects and worms. They are able to catch insects by flicking out sticky tongues very fast.

Frogs hibernate through the winter. When the weather becomes cold they bury themselves in leaves and mud at the bottom of a pond, and wait for the warm weather.

Frogs (2)

Frogs live on land or in water. In the early stages they are tadpoles, and breathe through gills. Their bodies change, and they develop lungs. As frogs they live out of the water, but return to it to prevent their bodies drying up.

Frogs eat small creatures. They catch insects by flicking out sticky tongues.

Frogs hibernate in winter. They bury themselves at the bottom of a pond, and wait for spring.

Remember:

● Using words you don't need makes things difficult to read!

● Sometimes words just say the same thing as other words (e.g. full-grown and adult). You only need one!

● Sometimes descriptive words tell you what you already know (e.g. cold winter).

● Be careful! Taking away too many words may make your writing sound like notes - or it may not make sense at all!

Person and Agreement

Following Behind (1)

I slipped out of the front door and looked down the street. There he was!

Quietly I shut the door behind me and walked after him. I hoped he wouldn't turn round and see me following him. I tried to be as quiet as possible, but once my foot hit a stone and it rattled onto the road. I slipped into a doorway. He turned round but I don't think he saw me.

We were soon into the brightly-lit streets. He stopped to look in a shop window. There was nowhere for me to hide!

Then I lost him. A bus came by. At the very last minute he jumped on. I wonder if he had guessed he was being tracked?

Following Behind (2)

Susan slipped out of the front door and looked down the street. There he was!

Quietly she shut the door behind her and walked after him. She hoped he wouldn't turn round and see her following him. She tried to be as quiet as possible, but once her foot hit a stone and it rattled onto the road. She slipped into a doorway. He turned round but she didn't think he saw her.

Following Behind (3)

Mike and Susan slipped out of the front door and looked down the street. There he was!

Quietly they shut the door behind them and walked after him. They hoped he wouldn't turn round and see them following him. They tried to be as quiet as possible, but once Mike's foot hit a stone and it rattled onto the road. They slipped into a doorway. He turned round but they didn't think he saw them.

Being Followed

"I knew you were following me! I saw you slip into that doorway after you had kicked that stone. . . ."

How to Follow Someone

To follow someone without being seen, you should . . .

Remember:

- Writing in the first person uses 'I' (one person) or 'We' (more than one).
- The first person sounds as if the character in the story is speaking (e.g. 'As I turned the corner I saw…').
- Writing in the third person uses 'he' or 'she' (one person) or 'they' (more than one). It sounds as if the author is telling the story (e.g. 'As they turned the corner they saw…').
- The second person uses 'you'. It shows someone is speaking directly to someone. It is usually used for instructions or questions (e.g. 'Now turn the corner. What can you see?').
- Make sure your verb matches the person (e.g. I am, we are).

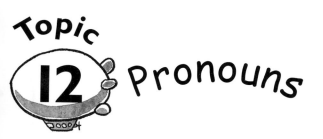

The Fish Family (1)

Mr and Mrs Fish had four children. Edith Fish, the eldest, had left school. Edith Fish worked in a bank in the High Street. Working in the bank was a good job and the family were very proud of Edith Fish.

Richard Fish was their eldest son. Richard Fish was quiet and dreamy and Richard Fish spent Richard Fish's time reading and thinking deep thoughts. Richard Fish was clever, but Mr Fish knew that working in a bank was not the job for Richard Fish.

Last came the twins, Celia and Marie Fish. No one called the twins that - the twins were just the Twins. The Twins were always together. The Twins' main interest was the family collection of pets. There was Basil the dog. Basil the dog was a weak, terrified creature and Basil the dog was terrified of Rosemary. Rosemary was a large and savage cat. Apart from Basil the dog and Rosemary the cat there were the goldfish. The goldfish lived in a large tank in the hall. The family joke was that the goldfish were members of the Fish family too.

The Fish family was a happy and normal family, and the Fish Family loved The Fish family's big family meals together.

But the Fish family never ate fish.

The Fish Family (1)

Mr and Mrs Fish had four children. Edith Fish, the eldest, had left school. She worked in a bank in the High Street. _____ was a good job and the family were very proud of _____.

Richard Fish was their eldest son. He was quiet and dreamy and he spent _____ time reading and thinking deep thoughts. _____ was clever, but Mr Fish knew that working in a bank was not the job for _____.

Charlie's Gang

Charlie Walker's gang was well known in the town. _____ had three members. Susie Slack was the brains of the outfit. _____ planned every operation, and made sure _____ were always a success. _____ planning never let the gang down! Sid Dark supplied the muscles. No-one wanted to meet _____ on a dark night. Finally came the leader, Charlie himself. _____ led every operation from the front.

P.C. Thomas did _____ best to tackle the gang, but without success. "_____ am really worried about _____" _____ said. " If _____ are not stopped now, imagine the problems _____ will have when _____ are old enough to go to school!"

Remember:

- Pronouns (e.g. **I, you, him, her, it, they**) take the place of nouns. Using them means you don't have to repeat the nouns every time you mention the thing they name.

- Pronouns can show belonging (e.g. *her* job, *their* tank, *his* time).

- Make sure that the verb matches the person (e.g. I *am*, we *are*).

Behind You!

The strange planet looked exciting, but Professor Ming would not let the crew rush out until she had checked that the air was fit to breathe. While they waited, Tim took photographs out of the window.

At last the professor agreed that they could open the airlock, and the crew rushed out. Because they had been in space so long, the sunshine was more welcome than usual.

Though it looked quiet outside Professor Ming had warned them to take care in case of danger. If wild creatures appeared, they would have to rush back to the ship, so Susy was asked to keep a lookout. She sat on top of a tall rock so that she could see in every direction.

It was a beautiful day on the mystery planet and the sun was very warm. Although Susy tried hard to stay awake, she soon dozed off.

While the crew were exploring, Professor Ming took samples of the soil and rocks. She was so busy that she didn't see the alien creeping up behind her, so it came as a big surprise when it tapped her on the shoulder.

Making Friends

Professor Ming was rather frightened.
The alien turned out to be friendly.
The crew came back.
They found the Professor and the alien drawing pictures on the ground.
They were trying to communicate.
It wasn't working.
The alien gave up.
He walked off.
Everyone followed him.
Professor Ming was worried that they might be captured.
They arrived at a village.
The aliens made them welcome.
They gave them food.
It was revolting!
They tried to eat it to be polite.

Remember:

● Conjunctions link short sentences to make longer ones. 'It was cold. I put on my coat' can become: 'Because it was cold I put on my coat' or 'It was cold so I put on my coat'.

● There are many different conjunctions all with different meanings, such as **and**, **but**, **so**, **or**, **if**, **though**, **while**, **until**, **when**, **since**, **that**, **because**.

● Choose your conjunctions carefully!

Topic 14 Time Sequences

A Walk in the Dark

As soon as it was dark, the cat pushed through the cat flap. He stood still for a moment, sniffing the air. When he was sure everything was as it should be he set off. First he checked along the hedge for any mice still searching for food. Next he had a sniff under the shed where a rat had once lived. After that he set off under the gap in the gate towards a little group of trees.

Just then there was a sound in the dead leaves. Immediately the cat stopped moving and crouched down. Very gradually he reached out a paw.

Suddenly something jumped straight out of the leaves. It was a frog! The cat had never seen one before and was startled by this strange leaping creature. Too late, he jumped, but the frog was out of reach.

When the cat had recovered from meeting this strange creature he set off once more down the path. At last he reached the trees. Surely there was something to catch here! Once he had caught a small bird that had fallen from a nest.

Nothing was moving under the trees. At last the disappointed cat turned for home.

Henry's Walk Home

It was a long walk home for Henry. He crossed the road outside the school and then followed the path by the side of the main road and then reached the railway line. Then he crossed over the railway bridge then set off up the hill to the church then found that the gate to the churchyard was locked then he wondered which would be the best way to get home then he decided to walk through the field next to the churchyard. Then he crossed over the stile and then he started walking across the field and then he noticed a bull in the field. Then the bull charged at Henry then Henry set off as fast as he could then he reached the gate and then he jumped over it to safety and then the bull got there.

Remember:

● You can use words or phrases to connect sentences in interesting ways.

● **As soon as, when, first, next, soon, later, that night, after tea, after that, finally** are examples of words and phrases that tell you when things happened. They are useful if you are describing a series of events.

● Don't just use **then** or **and then**!

The Very Special Pudding

Jane Stephens, head chef at the Grand Hotel, looked through her recipe books. Important visitors, business people from abroad, were coming to stay at the hotel, and she had to cook a very special dinner. She wanted to make something really exciting!

'I know,' she thought. 'I'll cook a special English pudding.' She found a delicious recipe containing apples, blackcurrants, ginger, brown sugar and nutmeg, all wrapped in pastry.

Although she didn't have to start until the evening, Jane decided to get prepared in good time. She would need a food mixer to make the pastry, a bowl to mix the filling in and a large baking dish in which to cook the pudding. She then checked she had the correct ingredients: apples, blackcurrants, spices and so on.

After tea, she started work. She peeled the apples, made the pastry, and started to blend the blackcurrants with the ginger spice. At last it was done. Carefully, she poured the fruit mixture into the baking dish, making sure it was all thoroughly mixed.

Suddenly, she remembered something she had forgotten!

The tin of nutmeg, which she had got out earlier, was on the table nearby. She grabbed it up, stirred in a spoonful, put the pastry over the top and popped it in the oven.

Just then Michael, her assistant chef, came along.

"I can't find my curry powder," he said. "I left it here on the table!"

The guests, who ate every bit, thought it was the most unusual pudding they had ever tasted!

What's in the Pud?

What's in the pud? What's in the pud?
Stir it round to make it good!

A pound of currants, a bag of flour,
Chinese spare ribs, sweet and sour,
Tomatoes, a dollop of Stilton cheese,
A pinch of pepper (please don't sneeze),
Some sugar that's brown, some sugar that's white,
Some peas, some sticks of dynamite,
Roll in a cloth, soak it in beer,
Bake in the oven until next year!

Remember:

Commas are used to:

- show where there is a break in the sense of a sentence.
- mark off extra information in a sentence.
- separate a clause from the rest of the sentence.
- divide up a list of nouns, adjectives or verbs.